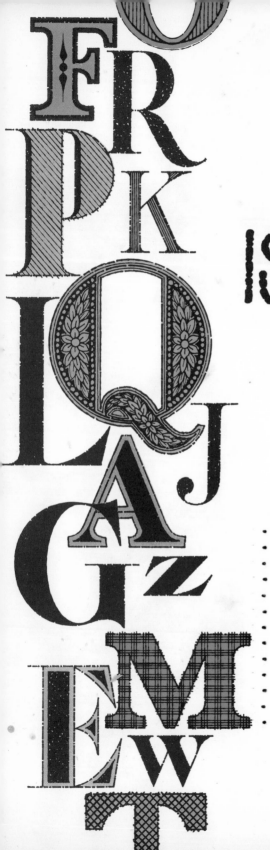

SPELLING MY NAME IS A GAME

conceived by
Freeman Gosden, Jr.

written by
Helen Petrie
Sue Schrager
Alan L. Taylor

designed and illustrated by
Paul L. Taylor

This book was written

especially for

Jennifer Weber

with love and kisses from

Mom And Dad

ISBN-0-915058-28-6

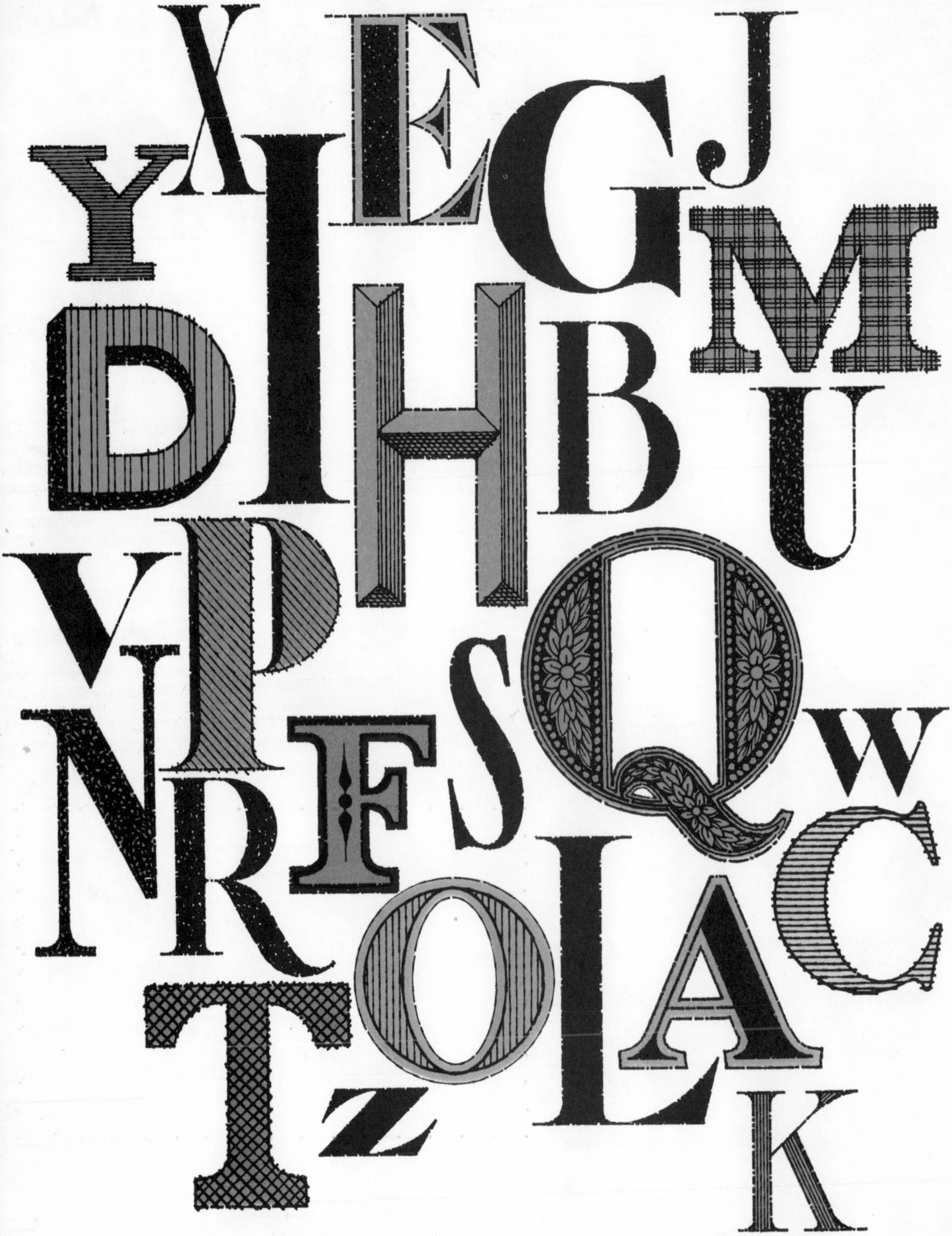

Look at all these letters, Jennifer!
When they are all placed together, they are
called the ALPHABET. When you use these
letters in the proper way, you are spelling
WORDS.

Everybody uses words. That's how you talk
to Brian, Dianna and Virginia.
You see words everywhere. This whole book
is full of words. That's how we read. Have
you seen any of these words?

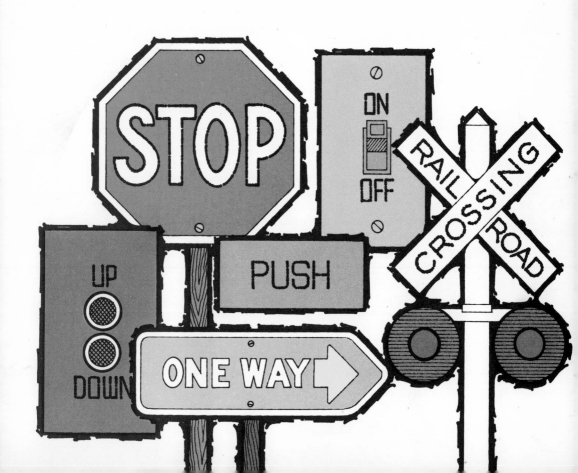

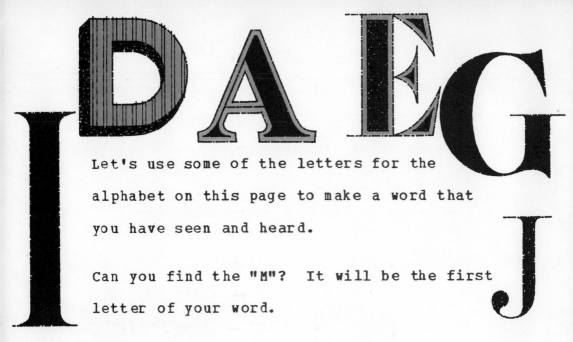

Let's use some of the letters for the
alphabet on this page to make a word that
you have seen and heard.

Can you find the "M"? It will be the first
letter of your word.

Now find where the "I" is. You can put it next
to the "M". It's a straight letter, isn't it?

The third letter we want to use is shaped like
this: "L". Can you find it?

The last letter for you to find and use in
your word is the "K".

What word have you spelled by putting all
these letters together?   ——"MILK"!

Do you like to drink milk?

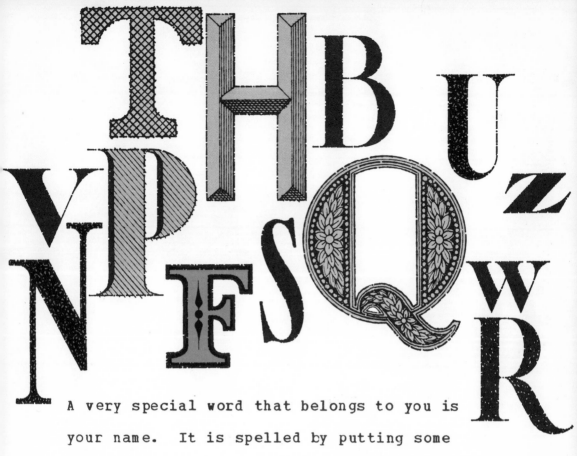

A very special word that belongs to you is your name. It is spelled by putting some letters together. We are going to use the letters on each page of this book to spell your name. Maybe we'll spell your city, too.

There will be a lot of fun things to do while you see your name being spelled. After you learn the letters in your name, you will be able to show other people what it looks like.

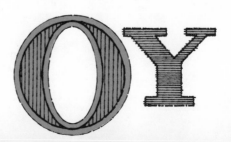

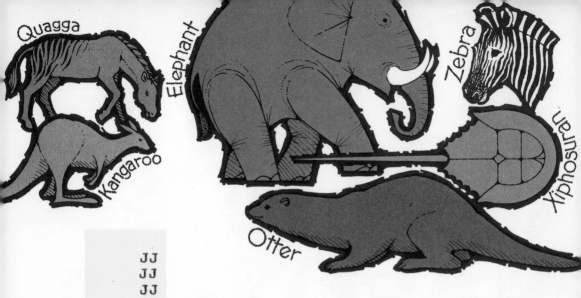

```
    JJ
    JJ
    JJ
    JJ
JJ  JJ
JJ  JJ
JJJJJJJ
 JJJJJ
```

The only place to start is with the
first letter of your name. You can
make this letter with your arms,
legs, and body. Try it! Can you find the
word and picture on these two pages of animals
that also begins with "J"? Some other words
that begin with "J" are Jig saw,
Jam, and Jackstraws. Is
this letter used in Brian, Dianna,
or Virginia?

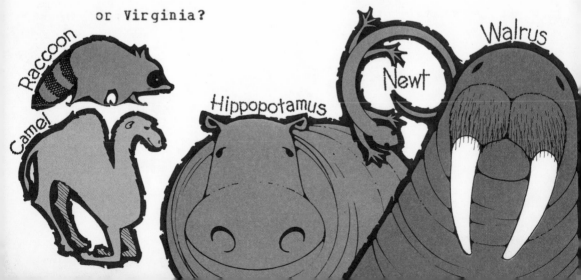

Carrots

Bananas

Apple

Ham

Eggs

Fudge

Grapes

Doughnut

```
EEEEEEE
EEEEEEE
EE
EEEE
EEEE
EE
EEEEEEE
E EEEEEE
```

The second letter in your name looks
like this. It is the first letter
of Elf, Escalator,
and Eye. Can you find a food that
begins with "E" in these pictures? Have you
ever eaten this kind of food?
Add this letter to your first letter. We will
keep adding letters as you turn each page until
you see your whole name spelled.

   J E - - - - - -   - - -

   J e - - - - - -   - - -

Jelly

Ketchup

Lobster

Ice Cream

Orange

Nuts

Meatballs

Xalpheffer

Waffle

Yam

Veal

Pineapple

Queen Olives

Zucchini

Upside-down Cake

Strawberries

Radishes

Tomato

The next letter in your name is "N".
This letter begins the words
Noodle, Newspaper,
and Nurse. Find the
flower or plant on these pages that begins with
"N". How many "N"'s can you find in the names
of these flowers and plants?

```
NN    NN
NNN   NN
NNNN  NN
NNNNNNN
NN NNNN
NN  NNN
NN  NNN
NN   NN
```

        J E N - - - - - - - - -

        J e n - - - - - - - - -

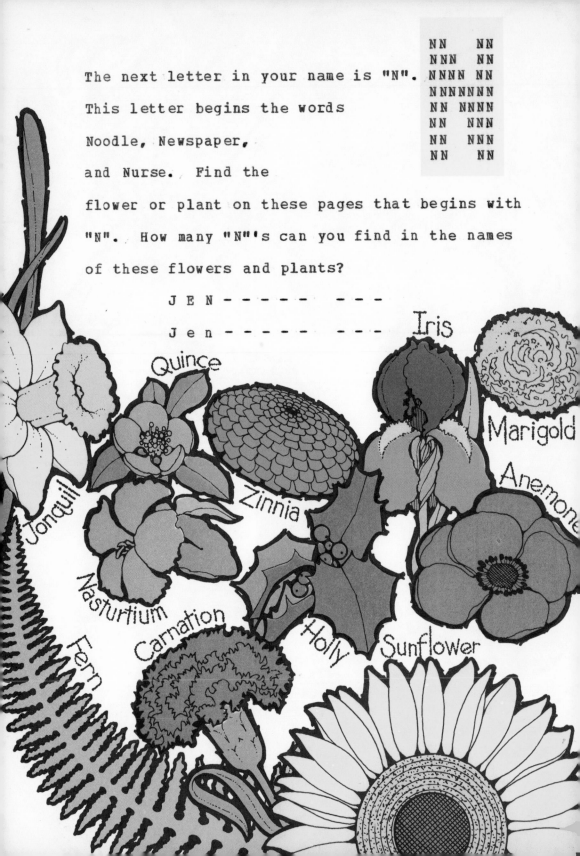

Iris

Quince

Marigold

Anemone

Jonquil

Zinnia

Nasturtium

Carnation

Holly

Sunflower

Fern

Lilac

Orchid

Xerophyte

Umbrella plant

Poinsettia

Violet

Buttercup

Rose

Water Lily

Tulip

Kumquat

Gardenia

Easter Lily

Daisy

Yucca

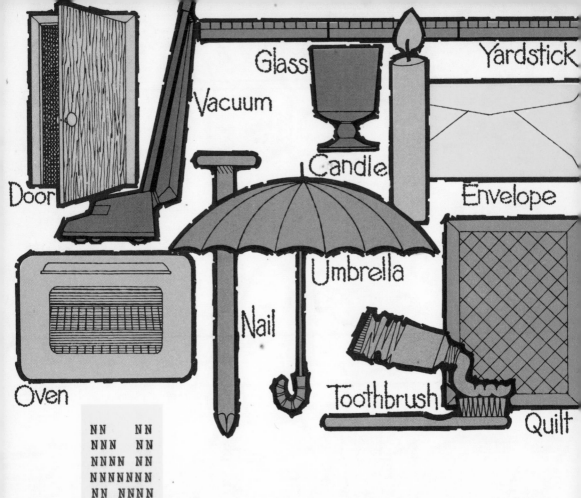

Glass

Yardstick

Vacuum

Candle

Door

Envelope

Umbrella

Nail

Oven

Toothbrush

Quilt

```
NN    NN
NNN   NN
NNNN  NN
NNNNNNN
NN NNNN
NN  NNN
NN  NNN
NN   NN
```

This is the next letter in your name. Does the shape of this letter remind you of something? Some words that begin with "N" are Nickel, Noon, and Napkin.

There is something around the house that begins with "N". Can you find its picture here? Can you find this letter in Silver City?

J E N N - - - -   - - -

J e n n - - - -   - - -

Armchair

Spoon

Zither

Jar

Knife

Hammer

Broom

Window

Pencil

Iron

Lamp

Radio

Faucet

Xylophone

Mirror

```
IIIIIII
IIIIIII
  III
  III
  III
  III
IIIIIII
IIIIIII
```

Add this letter to the letters you
already have. Trace this letter
with your finger to practice how it
is made. Inventor, Icicle, and
Ice cream cone all begin with "I". Find the bird
whose name begins with "I". Is there another bird
here that has "I" in its name? Can you name the
letters you have used so far?

J E N N I - - -   - - -

J e n n i - - -   - - -

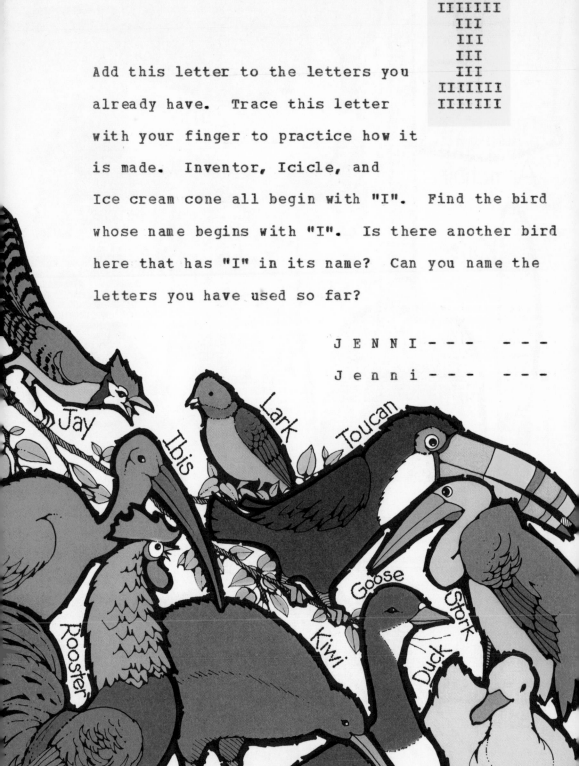

Quarry

Lighthouse

Circus

Underwater

Zoo

```
FFFFFFF
FFFFFFF
FF
FFFFF
FFFFF
FF
FF
FF
```

Try to form this next letter with
your fingers. Find the picture
for this letter. These pictures
are all places or things for you to go see.
Do you know some other words that begin with
this letter besides Ferris wheel,
Fin, and Factory? Count
the letters you have used so far to spell
your name. Are any of these letters used in
New Mexico?

J E N N I F - -   - - -
J e n n i f - -   - - -

X-ing

Elevator

North Pole

Volcano

River

```
EEEEEEE
EEEEEEE
EE
EEEE
EEEE
EE
EEEEEEE
EEEEEEE
```

The next letter for you to use is
shaped like this. These two pages
have a lot of children's names.
Can you find the one that begins with "E"? Is
it the same name as yours? How many names of
people you know can you find? "E" begins these
words: Explorer, Elk, and
Equator.

        J E N N I F E -   - - -

        J e n n i f e -   - - -

Roller skates

Zig-Zag

Volleyball

Ocarina

Wagon

Hopscotch

HOME

10 9 8 7 6 5 4 3 2 1

Golf

```
RRRRR
RRRRRR
RR   RR
RRRRRR
RRRRR
RR RR
RR  RR
RR   RR
```

This is what the next letter looks
like. Does it remind you of something
you have seen? Railroad,
Riddles, and Rhinoceros all begin
with "R". Find a picture of a game or toy that
begins with "R". Can you play this game?

Top

J E N N I F E R   - - -
J e n n i f e r   - - -

Archery

Quoits

Checkers

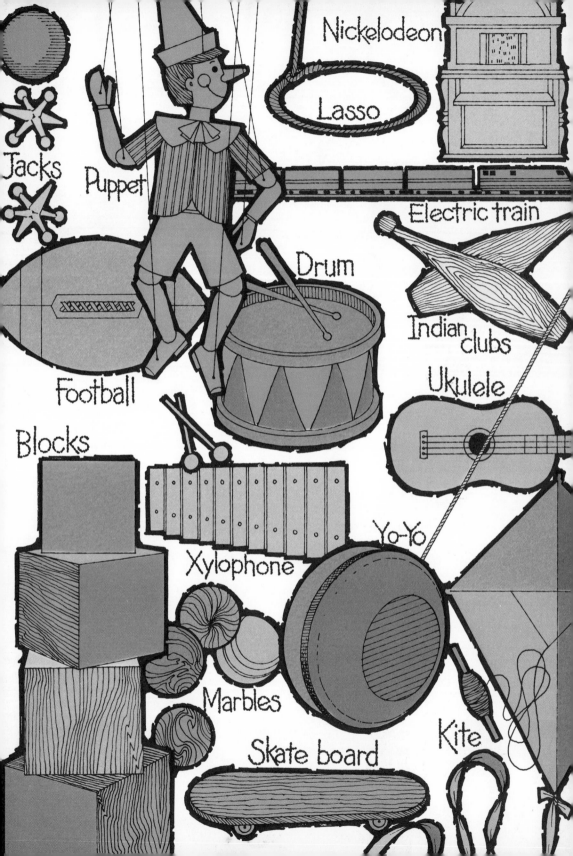

Jacks

Puppet

Nickelodeon

Lasso

Electric train

Drum

Indian clubs

Ukulele

Football

Blocks

Xylophone

Yo-Yo

Marbles

Skate board

Kite

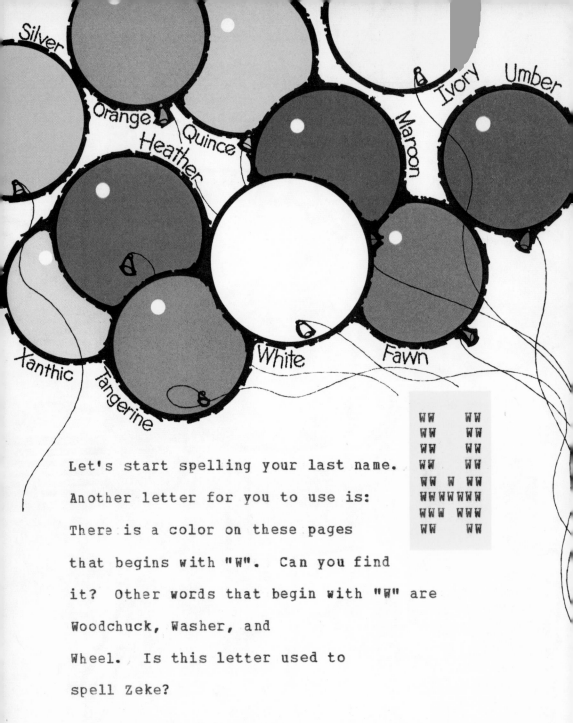

Silver

Orange Quince
Heather

Ivory Umber
Maroon

Xanthic
Tangerine

White

Fawn

```
WW        WW
WW        WW
WW        WW
WW        WW
WW  W  WW
WWWWWWW
WWW    WWW
WW        WW
```

Let's start spelling your last name.

Another letter for you to use is:

There is a color on these pages

that begins with "W". Can you find

it? Other words that begin with "W" are

Woodchuck, Washer, and

Wheel. Is this letter used to

spell Zeke?

    J E N N I F E R   W - -

    J e n n i f e r   W - -

```
EEEEEEE
EEEEEEE
EE
EEEE
EEEE
EE
EEEEEEE
EEEEEEE
```

Now we come to this letter:
Trace it with your finger.
Eyelash, Earth,
and Eraser all begin with "E". These
pictures show things you can wear. Find the
one that begins with "E". Is there a picture of
something you are wearing now?

Jumper

JENNIFER   WE-
Jennifer   We-

Windbreaker

Indian moccasins

Cap

Hat   Zipper

Pajamas

Xyloser

Apron

Belt

Shoes

Earrings

Overalls

Underwear

Gloves

Trunks

Necktie

Mittens

Vest

Yoke

Dress

Furcoat

Quilted robe

Knee socks

Raincoat

Laces

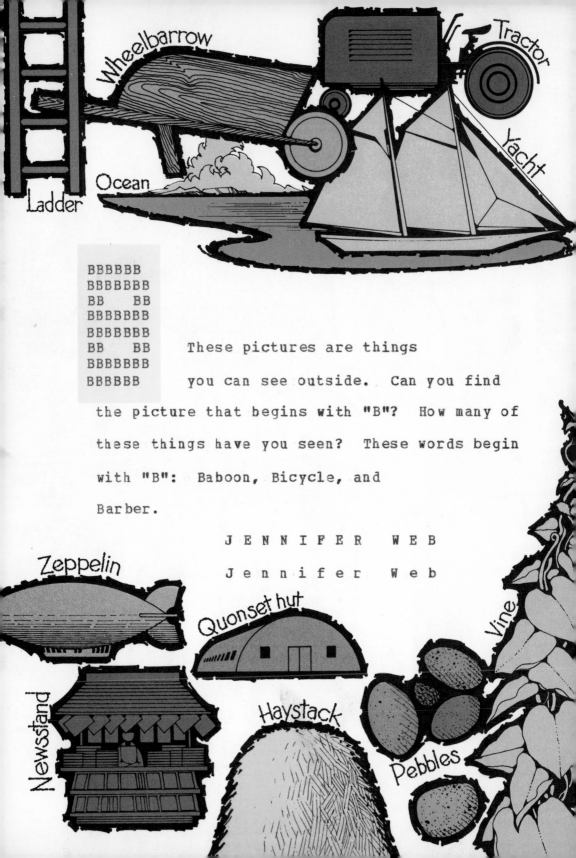

Wheelbarrow

Tractor

Ladder

Ocean

Yacht

```
BBBBBB
BBBBBBB
BB   BB
BBBBBBB
BBBBBBB
BB   BB
BBBBBBB
BBBBBB
```

These pictures are things

you can see outside. Can you find

the picture that begins with "B"? How many of

these things have you seen? These words begin

with "B": Baboon, Bicycle, and

Barber.

J E N N I F E R   W E B

Jennifer Web

Zeppelin

Vine

Quonset hut

Newsstand

Haystack

Pebbles

Bus

Engine

Drawbridge

Unicycle

Igloo

Kayak

Fence

Xat

Cabin

Sailboat

Jack-o-lantern

Mailbox

US MAIL

Rake

Anchor

Garage

Since you didn't finish spelling your last name,
you can complete it by finding a picture on
each page that goes with the letters you need.
Here's how your name looks all spelled out.

```
   J   EEEEE  N   N   N   N   IIIII  FFFFF  EEEEE  RRRR
   J   E      NN  N  NN   N     I     F      E      R   R
   J   EEE    N N N  N N  N     I     FFF    EEE    RRRR
J  J   E      N  NN  N  NN N    I     F      E      R  R
 JJJ   EEEEE  N   N   N   N   IIIII   F      EEEEE  R   R
```

Try spelling some other names, too. Let
Brian, Dianna and Virginia
play. Can you spell January or
Mom And Dad? And don't
forget Zeke.

Do you know your address? That's where you live. There are times when it is important to know this address: North Cooper.
You can start at the beginning of this book and play the game over again by using the letters in your address.

```
W   W   EEEEE   BBBB      EEEEE   RRRR
W   W   E       B   B     E       R   R
W W W   EEE     BBBB      EEE     RRRR
WW WW   E       B   B     E       R   R
W   W   EEEEE   BBBB      EEEEE   R   R
```

Now you know how to spell your name and address. What other words do you want to learn? You can have more fun with all the letters in the alphabet by using the groups of pictures in this book to spell more and more words.

Y X I E E G J J

D I H H B M M

V P S Q U

V P R F S Q W

N R F O L A C

T z O L K

How many other words can you spell?